CHOPIN

BALLADES FOR THE PIANO

PRACTICAL PERFORMING EDITION
EDITED BY WILLARD A. PALMER FROM THE ORIGINAL SOURCES

Second Edition
Copyright © MCMXCII by Alfred Publishing Co., Inc.
All rights reserved. Printed in USA.

Cover art: Le Boulevard des Capucines
by Colet Robert Stanley (1790?–1868)
musées de la Ville de Paris
© 1991 by SPADEM

D1413797

THE BALLADES

ABOUT THIS EDITION

Willard A. Palmer's *Practical Performing Editions* are subject to the same painstaking research as the well-known *Masterwork Editions*. To make fewer page turns necessary, editorial suggestions for the performance of ornaments are, for the most part, presented in footnotes. Parentheses are used to identify supplementary slurs, dynamic indications, etc. Fingering is editorial unless commentary in the footnotes states otherwise. It is hoped that this new series will fill the need for accurate, dependable, clearly engraved and economical editions.

THE BALLADES

Chopin was not inclined to append various romantic titles to his compositions, as was the practice of Schumann and Mendelssohn. The nearest he came to this is in the use of the title *Ballade* or "Ballad" for four of his larger works. The title is used, perhaps, in the sense of "Story" or "Legend," and each of these works is highly romantic in character. Each is also a product of Chopin's finest inspiration and craftsmanship. The title may have functioned to free Chopin from the obligation of the precise use of any definite classical form. Nevertheless, these works fall, though more or less loosely, into the category of the *sonata-allegro* form, particularly those in F major and F minor, with their clearly defined 1st and 2nd subjects.

The *Ballades* were composed after Chopin was 25 years of age, in the years 1835 to 1842, and all were published in three editions, the English, French, and German, during Chopin's lifetime.

It is not surprising, in view of their great musical worth, that the *Ballades* have become increasingly popular in recent years, and are now regularly featured on the programs of almost every concert performer of note, and are required fare for all serious students of the piano in conservatories and universities the world over.

ORNAMENTATION

THE TRILL *tr* and **ᴧᴧ**

According to the testimony of his own students, Chopin usually began his trills on the *upper* note. When the note immediately preceeding the trilled note is the same as the upper note of the trill and *legato* is indicated, the trill may begin on the main principal note, to avoid a break in the legato. This is in accordance with the rules of Muzio Clementi, whose methods Chopin used.

While the signs *tr* and **ᴧᴧ** were considered synonymous by C.P.E. Bach, Clementi and others, Chopin seems to have used **ᴧᴧ** most often to indicate the three-note *transient trill*, sometimes referred to as an *inverted mordant* (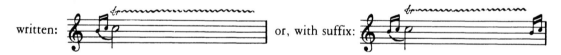).

For the *prefixed trill,* Chopin uses the following indication:

The second note of the prefix is not to be repeated, since the trill proper begins on the upper note.

When a short *appoggiatura* at the pitch of the main note is placed before the trill, the trill begins on the main note, on the beat. The starting note is not repeated.

written: played:

THE APPOGGIATURA

Appoggiaturas, single and double, are generally played on the beat. Exceptions are anticipations of the following note, octave skips, and those written before bar lines.

PEDALING

Although the modern pedaling indications are used, they are carefully taken from the original manuscripts and first editions, in which the older system (℘ ❋) was used. Overlapping pedal may be used at the performer's discretion.

Thematic Index

Ballade in G Minor

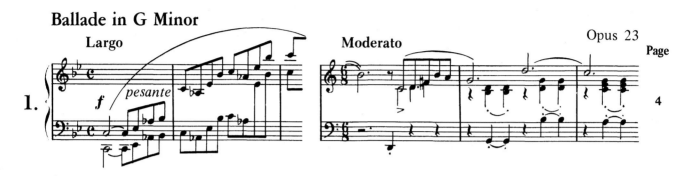

Ballade in F Major

Ballade in A♭ Major

Ballade in F Minor

Ballade in G Minor

to Monsieur le Baron de Stockhausen

Op. 23

(a) or with additional (faster) repercussions of the trill.

(b) The short *appoggiaturas* are played rapidly, *on the beat* of the following large note.

8

ⓒ Play the first of the two small notes *on the beat*.

Similarly in measure 123.

(e) Because one of the notes is an anticipation, this pair of small notes is played *before the beat*.

(f) The short *appoggiatura* (B♭) is played quickly, *on the beat*.

(g) The trill may begin on the principal note.

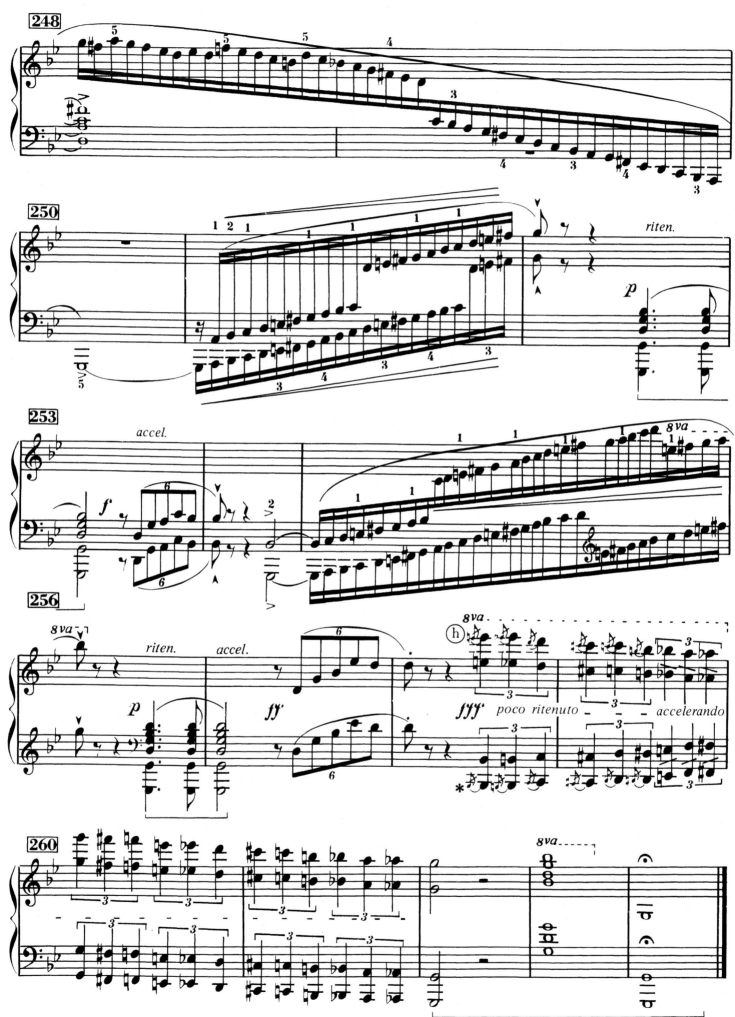

(h) Here the small notes are played *before the beat* of the following large notes.

Ballade in F Major

to Robert Schumann

Op. 38

(a) Similarly in measures 21 and 41.

Presto con fuoco

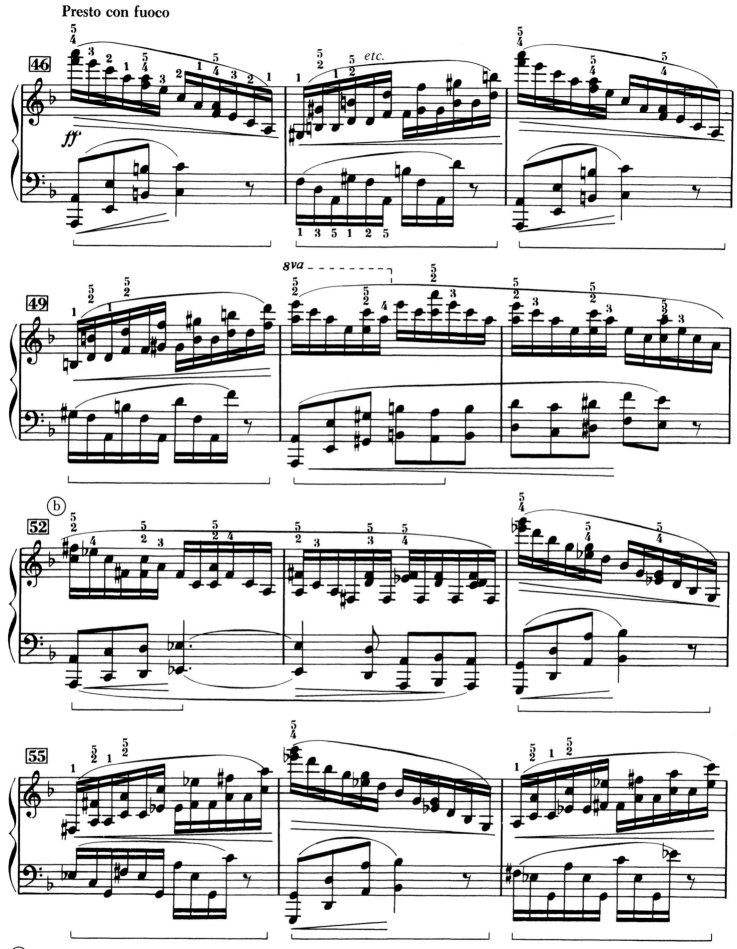

ⓑ The reading here is according to Chopin's final wishes, as indicated by a change he made on a copy sent to the engraver of the first German edition.

An earlier version has:    The 1st French and 1st English editions have:

stretto, più mosso

28

Presto con fuoco

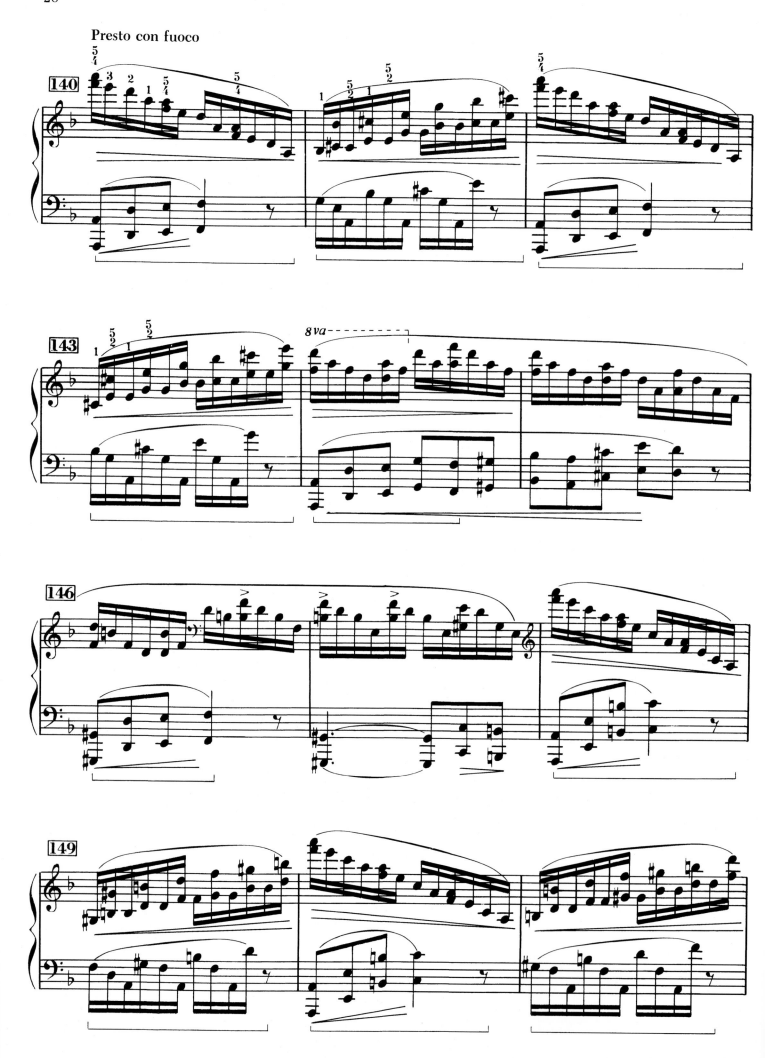

(c)
(d) These trills begin on the principal note.

(e) There are several versions of the last 3 measures.
Our text is taken from a copy corrected by Chopin.

Ballade in A♭ Major

to Mademoiselle Pauline de Noailles

Op. 47

ⓑ The small notes are played quickly *on the beat.*

ⓒ This and similar trills begin on the *upper note!*

34

(d) The short *appoggiaturas* are played quickly, *on the beat* of the following large note.

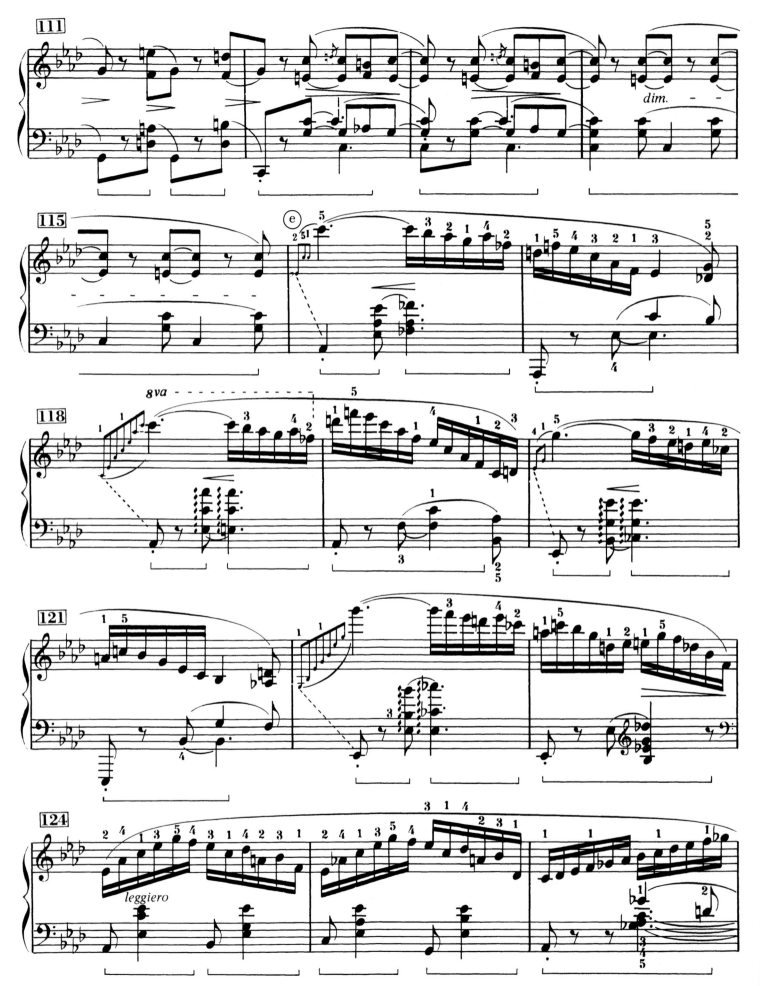

(e) Play the first of the small notes on the beat, together with the first
bass note of the measure, in measures 116, 118, 120, and 122.

Ⓕ The trills on this and the following measures begin on the *upper note*.

(g) The small note, being an anticipation of the following large note, is played *before the beat*. The first of the large arpeggiated notes is played *on the beat*. Similarly in measure 198.

(h) The small notes are played quickly, the first one *on the beat*.

(i) The trills begin on the *upper note*.

Ballade in F Minor

to Madame Nathaniel de Rothschild

Op. 52

Andante con moto

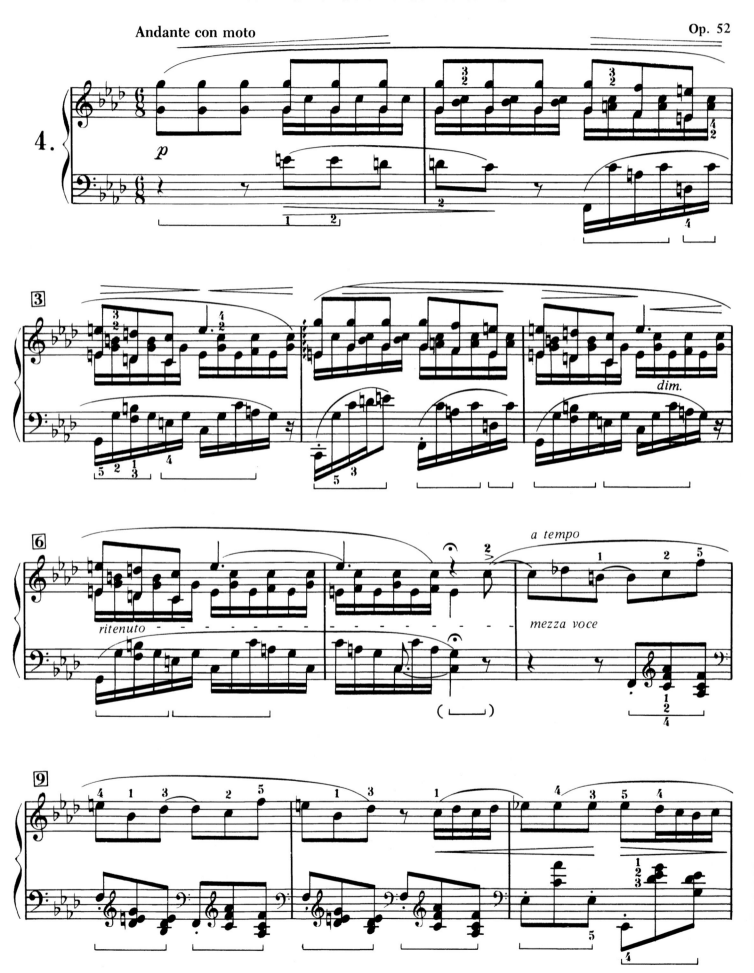

(a) The trill begins on the *upper note*.

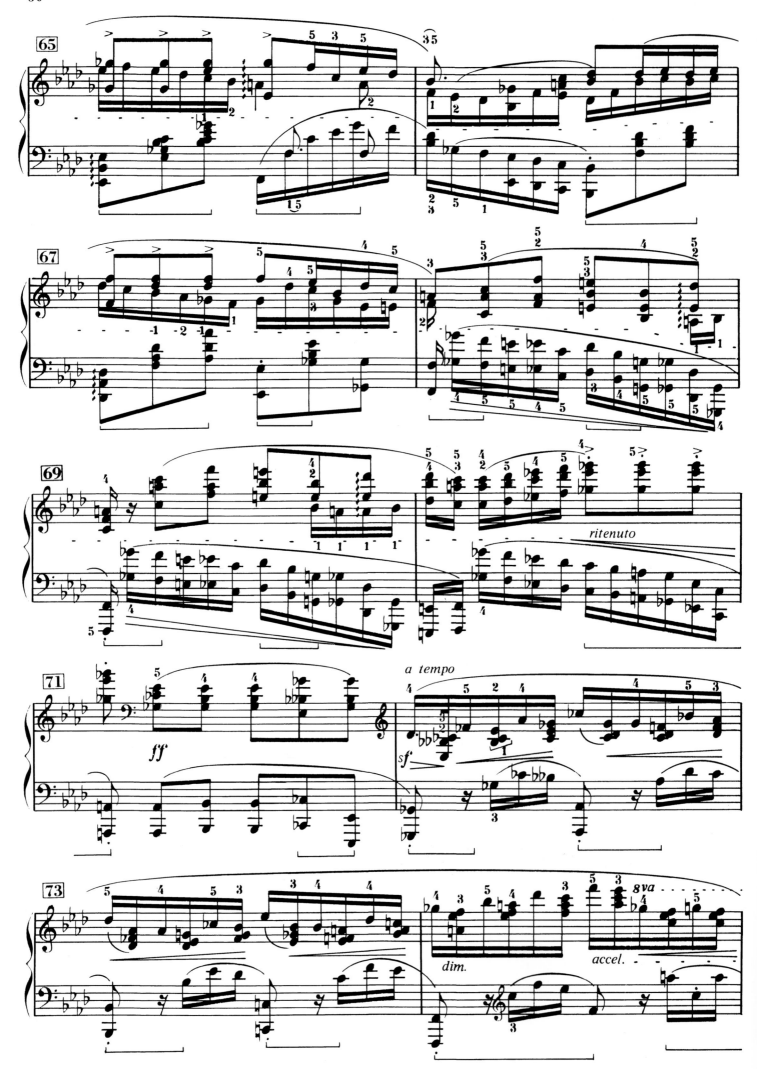

(b) The slur on the left side of this chord and the similar one in measure 93 probably indicates that the chords should be arpeggiated, approximately as follows:

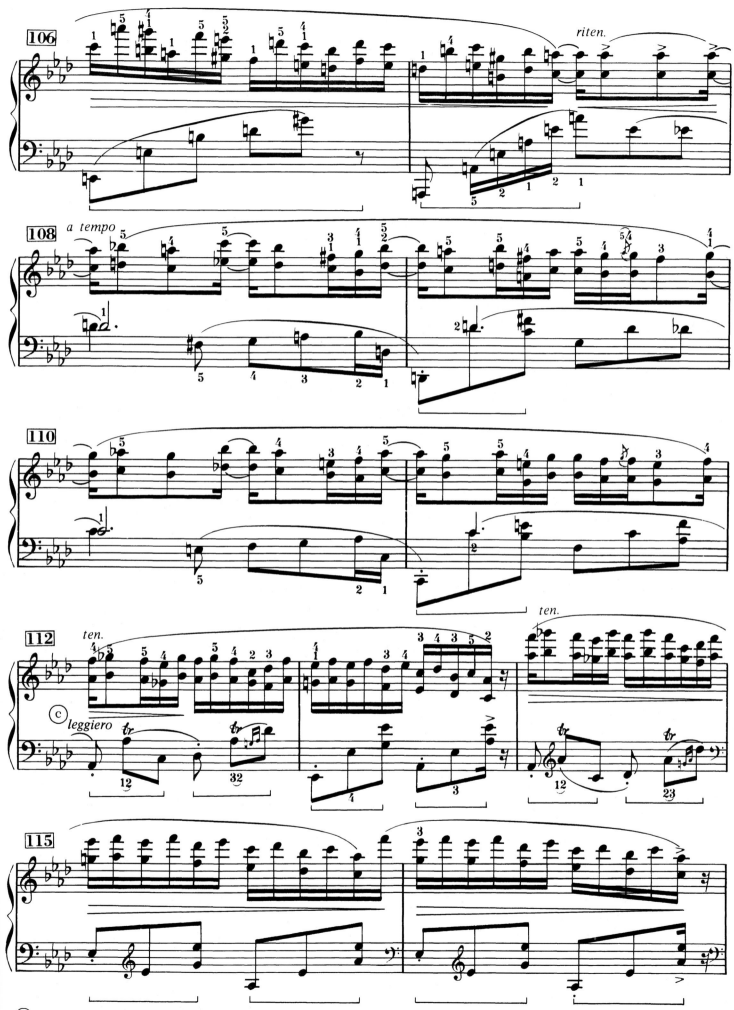

ⓒ The trills in this measure begin on the *upper note*. Similarly in measure 114.

54

ⓓ The trill begins on the *upper note.*

56

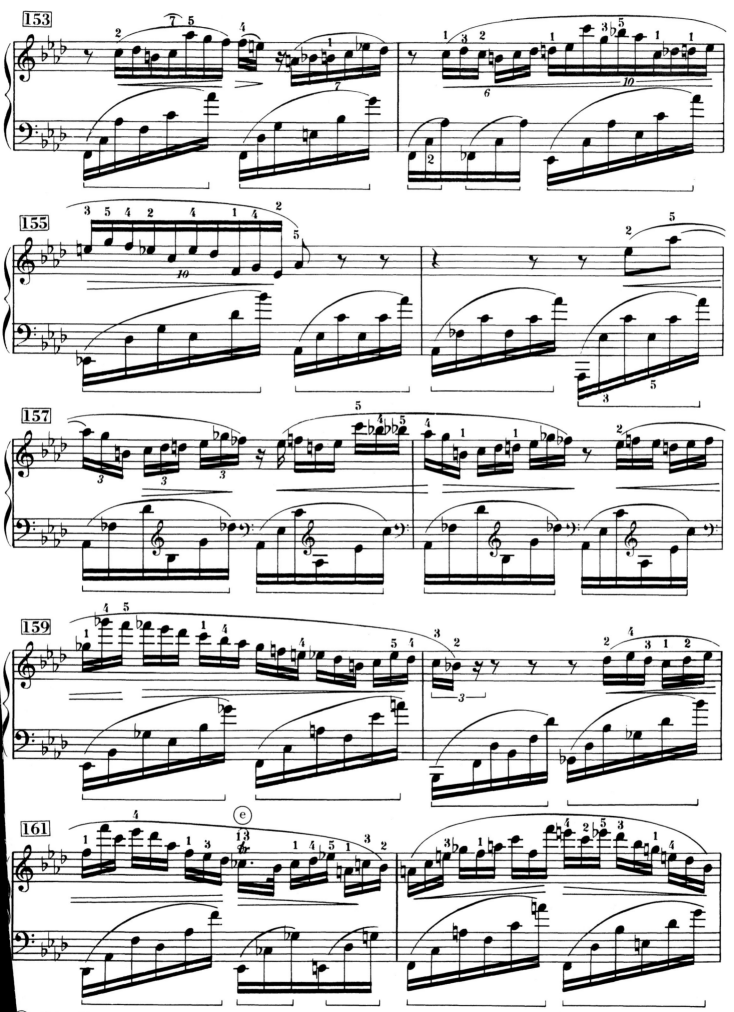

e) This trill begins on the *principal note.*

62